Those Kids in Proverbsville

D1518284

Those Kids in Proverbsville

By
Elizabeth Rice Handford

SWORD OF THE LORD
Murfreesboro, Tennessee 37130

ISBN 0-87398-823-X

Printed and bound in the United States of America.

Table of Contents

PROVERBSVILLE, U.S.A

Introduction

Proverbsville, U. S. A., looks like any other medium-sized town in America. It's those kids who live there that make the town so curious and exciting. You're looking at Proverbsville from Foley's Mountain. (Yes, I know it's a hill, not a mountain, and you know it's a hill, but the Proverbsville kids call it Foley's Mountain.) That's where Keith won the soapbox derby race last summer, but lost it because—

Oops! I nearly told you the story, and it isn't time yet. Later. . .you can see General Hospital over on the right. That's where Danny landed when he tangled with—oh, there I go again, nearly telling the story too soon.

Shubert's Creek runs along that valley behind the church. Proverbsville kids call it the Great Grey-Green Greasy Limpopo River, like in Kipling's "How the Elephant Got Its Trunk," since it runs through town and gets, well, sort of grey-green greasy! One time—aha! You'll have to wait for that story, too.

That's the Daily Journal building in the center of town. A newspaper office is a surprising place to find an eleven-year-old boy. How Teddy got there makes an interesting tale.

As you can see, Proverbsville is a city full of kids and stories waiting to be told, and that's what this book is all about.

I have to tell you (Though I 'spect you are smart enough

to have guessed it already) that of course all these stories have a moral to them. They're intended to help you build a strong Christian character. They'll teach you how good Christian kids ought to act in all sorts of hard situations. They'll show you the good habits God wants you to develop. I've chosen twenty of the most important of these and made up a story to illustrate each one.

The drawings for *Those Kids in Proverbsville* were drawn by Mr. Robert Danuser of Greenville, South Carolina. He used to draw Donald Duck and other cartoon characters for Walt Disney, but now he likes to use his pencil for Jesus.

Why is the town named Proverbsville? Because of the book in the Bible called Proverbs. God gave the proverbs to King Solomon to teach his little boy how to be a good Christian. There'll be a proverb for each story, and you can memorize it.

All set? Good. Paul and Steve were riding their bikes on a lonely trail nine miles north of Proverbsville. Paul's bike broke down. There was no telephone to call for help, no place to leave the bike, darkness is falling swiftly. What can they do? Find out by reading this exciting first chapter!

1. The Bicycle Sort-of Built for Two

Those Thrifty Kids in Proverbsville

"Steve, what time is it?—Hey, that's a nice watch. Where'd you get it?" Paul was scooping up a jumble of toys and books from the floor of his room, and Steve was waiting for him to finish so they could go to the ball game.

"This watch? Bought it at the school lost-and-found sale. It didn't work, but my dad showed me how to clean it. Look, if you don't hurry, the ball game will be over."

"Don't know why I have to clean up this mess anyway," Paul muttered, tossing a broken transistor radio into the wastebasket.

"Hold it—what are you throwing away there?"

"Old radio. It doesn't work. The case is cracked, too. May as well throw it away."

"Let's see if we can fix it."

"But the case is cracked."

"We'll use some Elmer's glue on it." Steve deftly unscrewed the back screws, lifted off the plastic case, and frowned as he followed a wire from the "on" switch to the battery. "Hmmm. . .broken wire. Listen!" He touched the two ends of the wires together, flipped the switch, and music blared out.

"Elmer's glue!" Paul mused, his eyes squinted with thinking. "So that's how you get all those things you've got. I know my dad makes more money than your dad does,

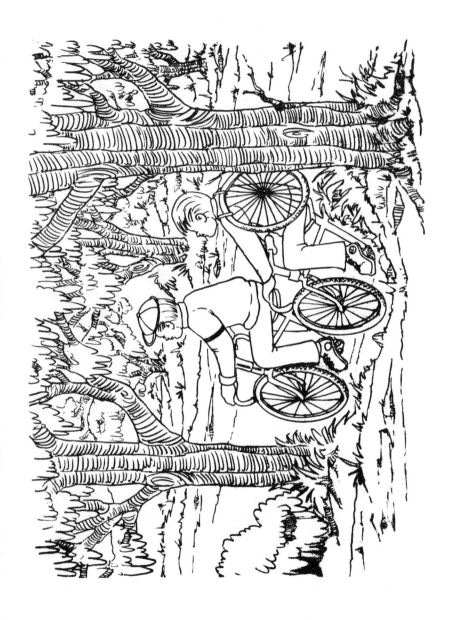

but you have all kinds of gadgets my dad says he can't buy for us."

"It's my father's philosophy—he says all the time, 'We'll make it do.' Like my bike. He bought it from a kid down the street, and found parts for it down at the junk yard."

"And my bike cost a hundred dollars!" Paul sighed.

"When you got that bike, I fussed, and Daddy made me memorize Proverbs 18:9: 'He also who is slothful in his work is brother to him that is a great waster.' Dad says it's as bad to waste good things as it is to be lazy—and once you start thinking that way, it's more fun to 'make do' than spend money!"

But Steve's ability to find a way to use what came to hand turned out to be more than just a neat little trick. It saved Steve and Paul from spending a hungry night in a very dark and lonely forest far from home.

They'd packed a lunch and slung a jug of water over the handlebars, and set out for the woods in the hills beyond Foley's Mountain. They had a wonderful day, finding all sorts of funny little forest creatures and strange fungus growths. They'd lolled under the sun in an open meadow, resting up for the nine-mile bike trip home.

"We'd better head for home, if we're going to be there before dark like we promised," they decided. But they'd hardly jumped on their bikes, and pedaled down the first hill, when Paul's front wheel hit a tree root. A piece of metal cracked sharply, and Paul tumbled onto the soft mulch of the forest floor.

The two boys looked somberly at the broken front wheel of the bike. "My new bike," Paul said, "and we're nine miles from home."

"Don't worry," Steve said generously. "We'll trade off, walking and riding."

"No, we'd be late. You ride ahead. Tell them I'm coming."

"Can't do that. You might get lost in the dark. Here, I'll pump you home."

"But somebody might steal my bike."

"Say—wait a minute, why couldn't we?—yes, we could. Here, put your front bar here on the back bar of my bike, like this," Steve said, hoisting the front end of Paul's bike to the back of his, and hooking the broken joint around the back post.

"But can we ride it?" Paul asked anxiously.

"Let's try it."

At first they wobbled and fell, but soon they caught on how the bicycle built for two should be ridden. And instead of spending a shivery night in the dark woods, they pedaled triumphantly into Proverbsville just as the sun reddened the western sky.

2. When Pigs Wear Diamond Rings in Their Noses

Those Discreet Kids in Proverbsville

Dorothy had a new pair of shoes, and Sally thought she would positively die if she didn't get a pair, too. "Oh, Daddy, they are black patent leather, and they have the cutest little velvet bow at the toe."

"Can't get them now, Kitten. So many folks have lost their jobs right now, they aren't buying much at the hardware store."

"Oh, but Daddy, you don't understand how cute these shoes are!"

"I'm sorry, Kitten. You have a nice pair of shoes. Be a good girl and listen to me. I cannot buy you shoes now. Business is bad. There is no money for frills."

Sally frowned. "Do you mean we are poor?"

Daddy shook his head, and tickled her under her chin. "No, Sally, not poor. We just don't have much money right now."

All night long Sally thought about it. They really were poor, and Daddy was just ashamed to say so! The next morning Sally told Dorothy all about it. It sounded so sad, tears rolled down her own cheeks as she told it! "We're poor, Dorothy. Business is bad, and we don't have money for food or clothes, or anything!"

Dorothy's black eyes widened. "Oh, Sally, how terrible!"

13

Sally's lower lip trembled. "I don't even know what we'll have for supper tonight!"

(Now that was true—she didn't know what they'd have for supper, but it was only because she didn't know what Mother planned, not because they had nothing to eat!)

Dorothy told her mother about it that night, crying. "Mother, the Moores are about to starve. They don't have any money, and nothing to eat."

"Are you sure, Dorothy? After all, Mr. Moore owns the hardware store."

"But Sally said that business was terrible."

"We must help them, then. They've helped so many others; we can't let them go hungry. I'll call Pastor Jenkins right now."

Pastor Jenkins could hardly believe it. "The Moores in trouble? Why, he gives his tithes every week. I don't see how business could get so bad so suddenly."

"Their Sally told my Dorothy they don't have a thing in the house to eat."

"Then I'll start to work on it right away. Our church family will certainly want to help them."

And they did. They streamed to the Moore house, their arms filled with sacks and boxes of food. Some of the men, when they shook hands with Mr. Moore, tucked an envelope in his hand. When he would open it, he'd be astonished to see money sticking out.

"What's happening? What is all this? Why are you bringing us all this food?" he asked, bewildered.

Pastor Jenkins patted him gently on the shoulder. "We know you are going through hard times, Mr. Moore, and we want to help you through it. We know you have nothing to eat. . . ."

". . .nothing to eat? But. . . ." Mr. Moore pointed

helplessly to the kitchen pantry, where the shelves were loaded with food.

"You don't need to be brave with us. We know you had nothing for supper tonight."

"Nothing for supper? What gave you that idea?"

Every eye in the room turned toward little Sally.

Her daddy looked at her with embarrassment. "Oh, Sally, what did you say?"

Sally began to sob. "I just said—oh, I wanted those shoes, and you said we were too poor to buy them now."

Daddy knelt down, and put his arms around her. "That's true, Kitten, but you knew we had plenty of food to eat."

"I know, Daddy—I didn't intend to say all that."

Mr. Moore looked around at the circle of loving friends. He smiled. "Thank you, everybody. Thank you very much. We'll find some people who really are poor to share all this with. Now, if you'll excuse me, I have an important Scripture to teach my little girl."

As all the people called goodbye, and left the house joyfully, Mr. Moore opened his Bible to Proverbs 11:22: "As a jewel of gold in a swine's snout, so is a fair woman which is without discretion." "Now, Kitten," Daddy said kindly, "you're a pretty little girl. But if you talk about private things that happen at home with people you oughtn't to, then you're liable to look like a pig with a diamond ring stuck in its nose."

"Yes, sir," said a very meek little girl, very thoughtfully.

3. When Mother Went to the Hospital

Those Prepared Kids in Proverbsville

It was nearly midnight when Kitty heard the moan. At first she thought it was the wind sighing in the trees. Then she realized it came from her parents' bedroom. Daddy was out of town. That must be Mother groaning. Perhaps she was sick!

Kitty jumped out of bed, not stopping even to put on her robe or slippers. "Mother? What's wrong?"

"Get me some water, please, Honey."

Kitty flicked on the lamp and gasped when she saw her mother's ashen face. Little beads of sweat covered her forehead. Kitty ran for the water. Her mother drank it, and lay back on the pillow, panting. Kitty felt her head. It was burning with fever. How could she get her temperature down? She ran for the aspirin, then washed her mother's face gently with a cool washcloth.

"Thanks, dear. That feels good."

"Shall I call the doctor?"

Her mother didn't answer. Just then Barbie started crying. Kitty went into her little sister's bedroom. She automatically reached into the crib, picked her up, dried her tears, and handed her a doll. Then she brought her into her mother's room. Anxiously, Kitty said again, "Mother, should I call the doctor?"

When her mother didn't answer, Kitty realized she'd

have to make the decision herself. Her fingers trembled as she dialed Dr. McClure's number. He came at once. He examined Mrs. Benson carefully. "Your mother is a very sick woman. We need to get her to the hospital right away. It's probably a gall bladder attack—we'll know for sure by the tests. Don't worry. She will feel better very soon. . . .Now, where did you say your father is?"

"In Minnesota. On a business trip."

"Can you reach him?"

"I can phone his secretary. She'll know where he is."

"Fine. Tell her to have him call me at the hospital. Now, let's phone for the ambulance. Let's see, you'll need someone to stay with you and the baby, too."

"Don't wrorry about Barbie and me, Dr. McClure," Kitty said bravely. "You take care of Mother, and I'll take care of things here."

"But you are far too young to be left alone here."

Kitty shook her head. "Ever since Barbie was born, Mother has been teaching me how to take care of her. She said some day there would be an emergency, and she wanted me to be ready. She taught me all kinds of things, how to cook and sew and clean the house, and everything."

Dr. McClure looked unconvinced.

"She's always quoting Proverbs 4:26 to me," Kitty argued, " 'Ponder the path of thy feet, and let all thy ways be established,' she always says. So she tried to teach me everything a girl needs to know. Honest, Dr. McClure, Barbie and I will be fine. You please just take real good care of Mother"—and for the first time a tear trickled down her cheek.

Dr. McClure put a kindly hand on her shoulder. "She will be all right, dear; you can count on it. And she will be very proud of the way you have acted tonight. You really were prepared for this emergency just like she wanted you to be! You're a mighty fine young lady, and I imagine you'll be ready for any other task life hands to you!''

4. Danny Does a Wheelie

Those Happy Kids in Proverbsville

"Hey, Rodney, have you heard? Danny's in Proverbsville General Hospital with a broken leg. I'm on my way to visit him now."

"Broken leg? What happened?"

"He was riding his bike to school, and a little kid stepped off the curb right in front of him. He swerved to miss him and hit a telephone pole."

"Well, he can't find anything in that to be happy about, I betcha."

"What do you mean?"

"Aw, that guy bugs me. He's always finding something to be cheerful about. One time we were playing with his electric race cars, and I gave mine too much power on a curve, and it shot right off the table. It smashed into a jillion pieces. I knew he'd be furious. But he wasn't. He picked up the pieces, and started examining the electric motor inside. Said he'd always wondered how it worked, and now was his chance to find out. He forgave me for breaking it!"

"Hmmm. Hadn't thought about it before, but you are right. Just last week—you remember how it rained so hard? Danny and I were going to the woods that day to build a dam in the creek and do some experiments and maybe fish a little. Then it rained buckets. I was almost

mad at God for ruining our fun. But Danny said we could have lots more fun in the rain. We could do more different experiments with the creek running high. He was right, too. We had so much fun!"

"He won't find much to be happy about with a broken leg and a smashed bike."

"Yeah, he'll be pretty glum. . . .I'll try my best to cheer him up."

But when Tommy got off the elevator on the seventh floor, he knew which way to go to Danny's room, just by the laughing and joking he heard. Sure enough, there was Danny, sitting in a wheel chair, and Dr. McClure and the nurse chuckling at something he'd just said.

"Hi, ya, Tommy! Come in!"

"Came to see you. Sorry about your leg."

"Yeah. Thanks."

"It must hurt awful."

"Oh, sometimes it gives me fits. But hey, Tommy, guess what I got to do?"

"What?"

"See inside the operating room. Dr. McClure let me see everything—the heart and lung machines and the X-ray equipment and the microscopes and operating tables, and everything. He taught me how to use the stethoscope, and how to take blood pressure. Why, I may decide to be a doctor instead of a scientist. What do you think?"

"But you can't walk or anything—"

"Yeah, but you'd be surprised at what this wheel chair can do. Why, I can even do a wheelie in it!" And Danny promptly jerked his wheel chair so the two front wheels hung up in the air for a while before thumping to the floor.

"But Danny, don't you feel bad?" Tommy asked.

"Sometimes it hurts pretty bad. Then I remember that verse our Sunday school teacher taught us. Remember? *'All the days of the afflicted are evil: but he that is of a merry heart hath a continual feast'*—(Proverbs 15:15). I figure the way to be happy is to think about all the good things God does for me. Then I don't have to make myself be happy. Happiness comes all by itself."

Tommy left the room, shaking his head. "Somehow I got it all backwards. I came to see Danny to cheer him up, and he cheered me up instead!"

5. Why Did Thurmond Howl in the Night?

Those Dependable Kids in Proverbsville

Johnny sat bolt upright in bed, awakened from a sound sleep. His heart was pounding fast. What waked him? Why was it so frightening? There it was again! Oh, it was only a dog howling. Why should that scare Johnny? After all, he was a big, strong, eleven-year-old, safe in his own bed in his own house. Why should a dog barking at the moon scare him wide awake?

Johnny rubbed the sleep from his eyes. He stretched, and his muscles creaked with soreness. He'd played softball for two days, and was stiff. He yawned, then wondered again, "What's wrong?" He looked at the clock. It was 4:30 in the morning.

Johnny leaped out of bed with a gasp. Now he remembered! Yesterday morning he'd promised old Mrs. Jones he'd feed her dog while she was away on vacation. But he'd forgotten all about the poor thing. Mrs. Jones had given Thurmond (what a queer name for a dog!) food and water before she left yesterday morning—but that was nearly two whole days ago. Poor Thurmond! How he must be suffering! What if he died because of lack of water? Johnny grabbed a pair of pants and pulled them over his pajamas.

Whatever had made him forget Thurmond? It was that baseball game yesterday. Mrs. Jones had phoned just when

it was Johnny's bats. He'd been so eager to get back to the game he'd said "yes" to everything without even thinking. Then he'd gone back to the game, and hit that home run, and in all the excitement forgot all about Thurmond. What if he were dead now? Or was that Thurmond barking?

Johnny tiptoed through the house, closed the front door gently, and raced down to the end of the block to Mrs. Jones' house. He unlocked the gate, closed it behind him, and squeezed his eyes shut so he wouldn't see Thurmond lying in a cold heap in the corner. But a forty-pound bundle of German shepherd leaped up on Johnny. Thurmond's yelp of joy and slobbering tongue told Johnny he was very much alive and O.K., even if a little thin and very thirsty.

Johnny filled the water bowl to the brim. While Thurmond noisily lapped up the water, Johnny fixed a huge bowl of dog food. Thurmond demolished the food, licking Johnny between gulps. Then Johnny filled the water bowl again. Finally, bulging like a water-filled balloon, Thurmond sank down by his doghouse with a sigh, and went to sleep. Johnny crept home to bed.

Later, he told Mrs. Jones all about it, of course, though he was ashamed. He knew he couldn't pretend he had taken good care of Thurmond when he'd gone for 36 hours without any water.

"All right, Sonny," old Mrs. Jones said testily, "I'll forgive you if you promise you'll learn Proverbs 25:13 and 19 for me: *'As the cold of snow in the time of harvest, so is a faithful messenger to them that send him: for he refresheth the soul of his masters. . .Confidence in an unfaithful man in time of trouble is like a broken tooth, and a foot out of joint.'"* Mrs. Jones pushed her glasses down on her nose. "Now, Sonny, do you want to be like a toothache to people?"

"No, ma'am, I don't," Johnny said earnestly.

"Then learn to be dependable."

"Yes, ma'am, I will." And Johnny set out to be dependable. He kept his promises. He did what he was told. If he said he'd do something, he did it.

And one day he got a wonderful reward. Mrs. Crawford called. She was a neighbor of Mrs. Jones. "Johnny," she said, "I have to go out of town for three weeks. I need a dependable boy to cut my grass, and forward the mail, and take care of my pet rabbits. Mrs. Jones says you are the most dependable boy in Proverbsville. Would you take care of things for me if I pay you $10 a week?"

Johnny grinned—not because of the money; he didn't even hear that part. He was busy enjoying the words, "Mrs. Jones says you are the most dependable boy in Proverbsville"!

6. Lucky—Lucky?—Stan Gets a Bike

Those Diligent Kids in Proverbsville

"Aw, Stan, it's too hot to work today. Let's call it off. Tomorrow maybe it will be cooler."

"Come on, Rick. If you work you won't be so hot."

"But look at that lawn. Did you ever see such a patch of weeds in your life? We can't get that all cut down today."

"Sure we can, Rick. Look how nice the part I've already cut looks."

"No deal. I'm leaving. You can finish it and keep the money Mrs. Crawford promised to pay us."

Stan shook his head, smiling as Ricky slouched down the street in his bare feet, his tennis shoes slung over his shoulder. Once before Ricky didn't want to help mow lawns because it was too cold. The week before, Ricky said it was too wet. The week before that, Ricky had been to Six Flags, so he was too tired to work. Though Ricky and Stan had formed a lawn-cutting partnership, actually Stan was the partner who had done all the work.

Stan shrugged his shoulders. Sure, cutting lawns was hard work. Sometimes you got real hot; some days you got cold. Sometimes the dogs nipped at your heels. Some days you had to pick up a broken bottle tiny piece by tiny piece. But Stan had worked anyhow, and now he'd saved $75.00 from his share of the work. Soon he'd be able to buy that big 18" mower, and then you'd see the grass fly!

He screwed his face, trying to figure the tithe he'd give the Lord from the $4.50 Mrs. Crawford would pay him for this lawn. His father had explained God would really bless his lawn business if he gave God His part first. Stan thought it would hurt to give away that much money, but he discovered it was a happy feeling to give money to the Lord to be used to help missionaries across the ocean, or the work of the church at home. And the money seemed to pile up anyway.

Let's see: one tenth of $4.50 is 45¢. Subtract that from $4.50: he'd still have $4.05. Add that to the $75.00 he already had—he screwed his face up more, figuring it all out in his mind—that made $79.05. Soon he would have enough to buy the new lawn mower!

The next week, when Stan had the new lawn mower, he phoned Ricky again. "Now you'll want to go into business with me, Ricky. This new lawn mower is really neat. We can cut Mr. Baker's lawn in 3 hours, I just know. Say fella, I really need help."

"Naw," Ricky said, licking his ice cream bar, "a doubleheader is on television today. I can't miss that."

Stan cut Mr. Baker's lawn all by himself, and so he got to keep the $6.00 Mr. Baker paid him.

All summer long Stan worked diligently, mowing grass, raking leaves, trimming bushes, pulling weeds. By the end of the summer, even after giving the Lord more than the tithe, Stan had enough money to buy a ten-speed bike. But it was no ordinary bike: it had a speedometer, a rear-view mirror, a headlight, tail lights, and turn blinkers!

When Ricky saw it, his eyes lighted up with envy. "Wow, Stan! You sure are lucky! I wish I could have a bike like that!"

"Lucky?" Stan thought to himself. "No, not lucky." He

patted his beautiful bike, and silently quoted a verse his mother had taught him at the very beginning of the summer:

"The soul of the sluggard desireth, and hath nothing: but the soul of the diligent shall be made fat."—Proverbs 13:4.

Poor Ricky! He was a sluggard—he was lazy, and used all kinds of excuses for not working. But excuses, no matter which ones he used, didn't get him the bike he wanted so badly. No, diligence and hard work—and God's blessing—were the way to get a new bike. Not luck. Not wishing. Just plain work.

7. When a Friend Lets You Down

Those Loyal Kids in Proverbsville

"Hey, something's all mixed up!" Becky thought, as she dodged the ball Martha deliberately kicked at her head. What in the world was wrong? Martha was supposed to be her friend. Why, they'd been friends ever since first grade. But now that new girl Lauri had moved to town, and Martha was giggling and whispering with her all the time.

"Oops," Martha smirked. "I'm sorry, Becky. The ball slipped."

It was sixth-grade recess. The girls were playing kick ball. Martha was a team captain, and usually she chose Becky to be on her team. But not today. She'd chosen Lauri. That girl had caused trouble ever since she'd moved to Proverbsville three weeks ago.

That first day Martha and Becky had a fight about Lauri. "We must be nice to her, Martha," Becky said. "She'll be lonely, just moving into town and not having any friends."

"Let her find somebody else. She'll try to break up our friendship," Martha argued.

"Nonsense, Martha. You and I will always be good friends."

"You just watch. Besides, Becky, have you noticed how she dresses?"

"Her folks are sort of poor, Martha. She can't help that."

"But she smells funny."

"That's because they heat their house with kerosene, and the smell gets into your clothes," explained Becky.

Martha wiggled her fastidious nose. "But all the other girls are avoiding her."

Becky's eyes clouded with tears. "That's why we ought to be extra nice to her. That's when you need a friend most—when you don't have somebody. . . . Besides, Jesus loves her, and so should we."

"Oh, I'll love her all right, I promise; I just don't want to be her special friend."

Ever since that day, Becky had been trying to get Martha to like Lauri, and Lauri to like Martha, but it was no use. Martha didn't want to share her best friend.

But today, suddenly, everything changed. Martha was best friends with Lauri, and Becky didn't have a friend in the class. She didn't like it, either, not one little bit. All the girls had laughed when Martha kicked that ball. Not one girl seemed to notice Becky needed a friend!

Just then, the kick ball came smashing across home plate and hit Becky in the head. It felt like those cartoons in the funny papers when somebody gets hit: she saw bright stars, and her head whirled. She blinked through her tears to see Lauri and Martha snickering. Lauri had thrown that ball on purpose to hit her! And Martha, who used to be her best friend, was laughing at her! "What kind of friend are you?" she cried bitterly.

Martha dropped her eyes and turned away. "I'm sorry," she said, ashamed.

Mrs. Caldwell, the teacher, came and put her arm around Becky. She checked to make sure Becky wasn't hurt, then said gently, "When we get back to the classroom, look up Proverbs 17:17. See if it can help you fix this problem.''

When Becky turned her Bible to Proverbs 17:17, she was really puzzled. "A friend loveth at all times, and a brother is born for adversity." "Mrs. Caldwell—you got it mixed up. Martha needs that verse, not me. She's not acting like a friend."

Mrs. Caldwell's eyes twinkled, like she knew a secret joke. "It's the right verse, and you're the person it's for. Think about it some more."

Becky stomped back to her desk. She thought, "The verse is true: a friend is supposed to love you all the time and not quit you when somebody new comes around. If everybody likes you, you don't need a special friend. It's when you are lonely and everybody is against you that you need a friend."

She chewed on her pencil still puzzled. Then all of a sudden her eyes widened. "Oh!" she said out loud, "I see!" The kids all turned to look at her. They grinned to hear her talking to herself. She smiled back at them, feeling her ears turn red. "I see, Mrs. Caldwell. I was wrong. I should have shown friendship for Lauri from the beginning, her being new and scared, and all. It was wrong to make Martha choose between us." Impulsively, Becky jumped to her feet and hugged Martha. "I'm sorry. I was wrong. Please be friends with me again."

She reached for Lauri's hand. "Count on me to be your friend, too, Lauri. I'm sorry I was snobbish."

A tear rolled down Lauri's nose and dripped on their clasped hands. Lauri sniffed, and wiped it off. Then she reached for Martha's hand and squeezed it, too. She didn't say a word—but then she didn't need to. Sometimes true friends understand each other without saying a word!

8. The Girl Who Had Everything

Those Caring Kids in Proverbsville

"Beat you to the end of the pool!" Virginia challenged.

"Oh, no you won't," Melissa answered gamely. But she knew she would. Virginia always did everything better than Melissa. The two girls dove. Melissa churned away, arms and legs flailing. Virginia swam by her with swift, sure strokes, leaving hardly a ripple in the clear blue water.

At the edge of the swimming pool, Virginia grabbed her robe. "I'll go get our lunch, Melissa, and bring it to the picnic table on the patio."

"Can I help?"

"Nope, you're a guest. Besides, Mother has it all fixed. Just get dressed, and we'll be ready to eat in a jiffy."

Virginia combed out her hair and walked toward the big house. Melissa's eyes followed her enviously. Virginia had everything. . .a big house, an important father, a swimming pool in the back yard. And she could do anything she tried. . .tennis, swimming, track. She was smart in school, too. She got good grades. She sang in the chorus. She got the best parts in the school programs.

Then Melissa's eyes clouded. Just last Sunday her Sunday school teacher had said, "Kids, don't forget the most important thing in the world is to know your sins are forgiven. It doesn't matter how smart you are, how rich you are, how strong you are, if you don't know you are

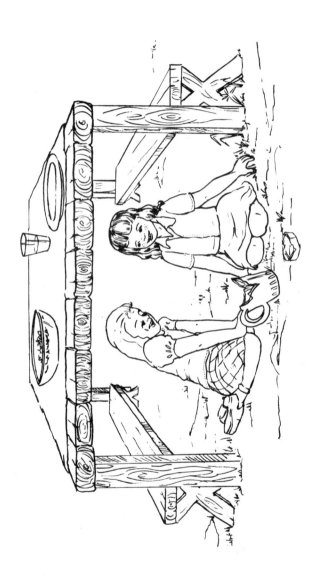

saved. You have a friend that needs Jesus. Her money, her talent, her smartness, won't save her from Hell." Then the teacher opened her Bible and read Proverbs 11:30: "The fruit of the righteous is a tree of life; and he that winneth souls is wise."

Melissa shivered. How could she, dumb and awkward, tell Virginia she needed anything?

Suddenly she realized she'd been waiting for Virginia a long time. Where was she? Melissa went to the patio. The lunch was on the table. But where was Virginia? She peered through the kitchen door screen. "Mrs. Jacobs, where is Virginia?"

"Why, I don't know, Melissa. Outside, I think. She was here just a minute ago."

Melissa went back to the empty patio. Virginia just wasn't there. Then Melissa heard a muffled sob. Someone was crying. Could it be Virginia? Melissa stooped and looked under the table. There sat Virginia, surrounded by the shattered pieces of a beautiful crystal pitcher. "Oh, Virginia, are you hurt?"

"No," she sobbed, "I'm so ashamed. Mother told me not to use that pitcher. It's old, and valuable, and she likes it especially. I was real mean to her, and said of course I wouldn't break it, and now it's in a million pieces, and why am I so bad?"

Melissa crawled down under the picnic table and put her arm around Virginia. And Melissa, the girl who couldn't do anything very well, told Virginia, the girl who could do anything, the one thing she needed. "Virginia, everybody does wrong. The Bible says so. But you can't get into Heaven by yourself, because God hates sin, and says it has to be paid for. But, Virginia, He loves you, too, and wants you to go to Heaven. So you know what He did? He let

Jesus pay for all your dirty sins for you. So why don't you tell Jesus you're sorry for all the bad things you do, and ask Him to forgive you for all your sins so you can go to Heaven?"

That day, under the picnic table, Virginia did ask Jesus to forgive her for all her sins. And Melissa learned there was one thing she could do, and that is tell kids how to get to Heaven. That, after all, is more important than anything else in the whole wide world!

9. Who Should Todd Really Be Afraid of?

Those Reverent Kids in Proverbsville

"Hey, Todd, wanna have some fun tonight?"

"Me? You want me with you guys?" For weeks Todd had wished Jeff and his friends would let him in their gang. They had so much fun together—at least they talked about all the fun they had. Todd knew they weren't Christians just by their language. But it was hard not to envy them—they got to do so many grown-up things. "Sure I want to have some fun. What do you have in mind?" he answered.

Jeff grinned slyly. "Fun. Of course, you don't have to come, if you don't want to."

"Oh, I want to."

"Can you keep your mouth shut?"

"Sure."

"Meet us in the garage behind Old Man Brown's house. Ten o'clock."

Ten o'clock? Todd flushed. He couldn't leave the house at 10:00. He'd have to sneak out. But that would be easy, because his parents trusted him. Todd wrinkled his nose. He didn't like to deceive his parents.

Jeff saw his expression and sneered. "Fraidy cat, aren't you?"

"No," Todd said hastily. "I'll be there."

That night at 10:00 Todd nervously pushed open the

41

door of Old Man Brown's garage. Its rusty hinges squeaked. He peered inside. Jeff waved an opened bottle of whiskey at him. He laughed when it slopped over the side. "Come in, Todd. Here's a bottle for you."

"Whiskey! Where did you get it?"

"It's my old man's. I swiped it out of his desk drawer."

"Here," Mike called. "Have a cigarette. We're really living it up tonight!"

Todd felt shame creep up his neck and color his cheeks scarlet. So that was the kind of fun they'd planned—stolen whiskey and cigarettes. He should have known better! Todd could almost hear his father's quiet voice quoting that verse he'd taught him: "Let not thine heart envy sinners, but be thou in the fear of the Lord all the day long. For surely there is an end; and thine expectation shall not be cut off" (Prov. 23:17,18). He'd envied the fun these sinners were having, when he should have been fearing God. And look where it landed him!

"I'm sorry, fellows," he mumbled. "I guess I won't stay."

"Hey, now wait! The fun's just beginning."

Todd shook his head. "No, but thanks anyway."

Jeff grabbed his arm. "You aren't going to squeal on us, are you?"

Todd gulped. "Not if you go confess it to your dad."

Jeff snarled, "You just try squealing on us, buddy, and see what you get."

Todd stumbled home. He woke up his father and told him the whole miserable story. "I'm sorry, Dad. It was a stupid thing to do. Now what am I going to do?"

Father's voice was gentle. "You did the right thing, Todd. I'm grateful. But we do need to tell Jeff's dad. Leviticus 5:1 says, 'If a soul sin, and hear the voice of swearing, and is a witness, whether he hath seen it or known of it, if he do not utter it, then he shall bear his iniquity. . . .' I'll tell you what. I'll phone him."

But Jeff's father thought the whole thing hilarious. "That kid stole all my liquor, did he? I didn't know he had it in him. Just butt out, Mr. Clark; he can take care of himself."

Todd tossed restlessly all night. Through his mind tumbled many thoughts: how grateful he was for his dad; how ashamed he was that he'd envied those wicked boys and been tempted to be like them; how glad he was that God was holy and rewarded people for doing right.

His father woke him the next morning with the morning paper. "GARAGE FIRE INJURES FOUR!" the *Daily Journal* headline said. "Four teenagers suffered from smoke inhalation and first degree burns last night when the garage where they were having a party caught fire. Police conjecture the fire started accidentally from a cigarette, and that the young men had been drinking so were unable to get out of the blazing building. Jacob Brown, owner of the garage, heard their screams and saved their lives."

"Wow!" Jeff whistled softly. "Thank you, Lord, for helping me to make the right decision last night. Help me never again to envy anybody who's doing wrong. Help me be afraid to displease You."

10. Who Messed Up the Pioneer Village?

Those Truthful Kids in Proverbsville

Susie spent hours looking at the quaint Pioneer Village Miss Thompson's sixth-grade class was making. It was so real, you could almost see the pioneers actually moving around the tiny log cabins. Sally's daddy had made a big sand table. Each child in the class had built a log cabin, or a barn, or a tool shed, or a tiny church to show what it was like "in the olden days." Steve made a blacksmith shop, with a tiny forge (the fire inside was really tin foil) and an anvil. He bent paperclips to look like horse shoes, and hung them on the wall. Eric made a canvas-covered wagon, filled with tiny barrels and boxes. Susie had made a spinning wheel out of florists' wire, and twisted a fluff of cotton on the end to show how it worked.

There were heaps of work to be done: the fence had to be finished so the cattle wouldn't wander out on the prairie and get captured by the Indians. (Hey, maybe they should make an Indian teepee village on the side!) They needed to make a road out of small stones. And Chris wanted to move some of the buildings so he could make a stream go right through the village, and power a corn mill. He thought he could use real water and make the water wheel turn. But the children voted against it—they didn't want to move their buildings, just in case they'd all collapse!

One noon, in the lunchroom, Miss Thompson was

telling another teacher about their project. "Susie, would you please go to our classroom? Get the book we're using for our guide for building the Pioneer Village. Do you know where it is on the shelf?"

Susie ran to the room and pulled down the big book. To her horror, the big book next to it flopped out, and smashed into splinters their beautiful Pioneer Village!

"Oh, no!" Susie wailed. She grabbed up the book. But the town looked like it had been flattened by a tornado! Susie looked out the door. No one was there. Nobody had seen. Quickly Susie poked the sticks of fence back into the sand. With fumbling fingers she heaped together the little wood logs that had been the blacksmith shop. Desperately she smoothed out the sand, and straightened the other buildings as best she could. Then she turned out the light, shut the door, and hurried back to the lunch room with the book.

Miss Thompson looked at Susie's flushed face. "Are you all right, honey?"

Susie dropped her eyes. "Yes, ma'am." But she was very quiet all the rest of the day. She kept holding her breath until someone would shout, "Look what happened to our Pioneer Village!" But it wasn't until the next day, when the class started their social studies, that they noticed the ruin.

"Who did it?"

"Why would someone do such a wicked thing?"

"Did the janitor do it?"

"If it was an accident, why didn't they say so?"

Miss Thompson sent every child to his seat. She asked each one, "Did you do it?"

Each child answered solemnly, "No, ma'am."

Susie thought she would choke on the words, but she said, "No, Miss Thompson."

"Children," Miss Thompson said solemnly, "we can repair the village, with some hard work. And I could let the whole matter go. But for the sake of the child who did wrong, I must ask you to think about it. I feel sure it happened accidentally. The class will forgive you for it, I know. But God does not want you to lie to cover up an accident. 'Lying lips are abomination to the Lord: but they that deal truly are his delight,' God says in Proverbs 12:22. Now, does anyone have anything to say?"

"I did it!" Susie blurted out. "Oh, I'm so sorry—I didn't intend to do it—but I should have told you, Miss Thompson. I did it when I got that book for you. A book fell on it. Oh, I am sorry!"

Kathy and Mary jumped out of their seats, and threw their arms around her. "Don't cry, Susie. It's O.K. We forgive you—all of us forgive you. Hush! Don't say another word!"

And nobody did. Quietly and carefully the class began to rebuild the little village. In a way, they were glad it happened. Chris got to move the buildings, and make a little stream—with real water!—run through the village and over the water wheel at the mill. But the happiest child in the whole room was Susie, who told the truth even when it hurt, and was forgiven for it.

11. When Donnie's Bum Leg Kept Him Out of the Club

Those Fair Kids in Proverbsville

Todd, Donnie, and Larry organized a secret club. They hadn't decided what kind of club it would be yet. They might investigate for enemy spies (though it didn't seem likely there was anything important in Proverbsville that enemy spies would want to know.) They might make it a scientific investigating club (after all, they had a telescope to look at the moon, and a magnifying glass that makes your skin look all bumpy and weird.) Maybe they'd explore something, or climb a mountain nobody had ever climbed before. (That prospect was a little dismal, considering Foley's Mountain was the highest point in Proverbsville, and little kids rode their tricycles up it!)

Actually, the purpose of the club wasn't too important. What they had to have was a clubhouse. It needed to be real private, so nobody could sneak in. It needed to be big enough for all three of them, and maybe another kid or two (boys, that is. Girls, never!)

Mr. Brown told them they could salvage the lumber from his old garage that burned last month. And Todd's daddy told them they could build a tree house in their back yard. So the three boys hacked and sawed, and finally got a nice pile of lumber for their clubhouse. It wasn't until they started carrying the lumber the two blocks to Todd's house that the trouble started.

"Todd," Larry said, "this is my third trip, and your third one. Don is still on his first load."

"Aw, Larry, you know why he's slow. He had polio, and he can't walk very well on his bad leg."

"It's not fair for us to have to do all the work."

"He's working as hard as he can."

"Huh! One load!"

"But Don's the one who figured out how we could cantilever the floor joists and make our clubhouse bigger."

"It's wrong for him to be in the club if he doesn't do his share of the work. If you don't work, you don't eat. The Bible says so."

Todd puckered his lips, thinking. "Yeah, but you're supposed to treat other folks like you want them to treat you, too" (Luke 6:31).

By this time Don had caught up with the boys. When he realized what Larry was mad about, his shoulders slumped. It always seemed to turn out that way. Nobody wanted him on their side because of his bum leg. "Never mind, Todd, I understand," he mumbled. He threw his load of lumber down at the foot of the tree, and walked over to his own yard. He lay down on the grass, and watched the boys continue the work. They'd started the tricky job of carrying the boards up the tall ladder into the tree. It was heavy work, and scary.

Todd kept trying to catch Larry's eye, but Larry ignored him. Being a Proverbsville kid, Larry should have remembered Proverbs 11:3: "The integrity of the upright shall guide them: but the perverseness of transgressors shall destroy them." "Integrity" is a big word that means doing right, being fair, all the time, and never taking advantage of somebody because they are weak. I wonder why Larry didn't remember that?

"Whew!" Todd said. "Let's stop a minute. I'm tired."

"Hey, fellows," Don called timidly. "I've got an idea. Todd, doesn't your dad have a big rope? I could climb up in the tree, and you guys could tie a couple of boards on the rope, and I could haul it up, and that way nobody would have to climb the ladder up and down."

"Great idea," Larry said. Then he blushed. "Would you. . .will you help us?"

"Yeah, Don," Todd added, "we need you in our club just for your brains. Will you come back?"

"I'm a pretty good lifter, too," Don said happily, as he scrambled up the ladder.

12. Who Will Win the Talent Contest?

Those Teachable Kids in Proverbsville

"Try playing those notes again, Nancy," Mrs. Thompson said severely. "You smeared them. Let me hear every note in the run."

"Yes, ma'am," Nancy said meekly. She played the passage again.

"That's better, but not good enough. Practice that run ten times a day every day. You'll be scared the night of the talent contest. I want your fingers to know this piece so well it doesn't matter how scared you are—your fingers will play it right anyway. Now start at the top of the page. Make this trill start softly, then get louder at the end of the second measure."

"Yes, Mrs. Thompson," Nancy sighed. It seemed like the piano lesson would never end. When Mrs. Thompson finally released her, she slid off the piano bench gratefully. "Your turn," she said to her friend Judy, who was waiting for her lesson.

"Old battle-axe," Judy fumed through clenched teeth. "She'd better not fuss at me like that."

Nancy grinned at her, but blinked back the tears.

On the way home after their lesson, the girls talked it over. "Nobody's going to talk to me the way Mrs. Thompson does," Judy said.

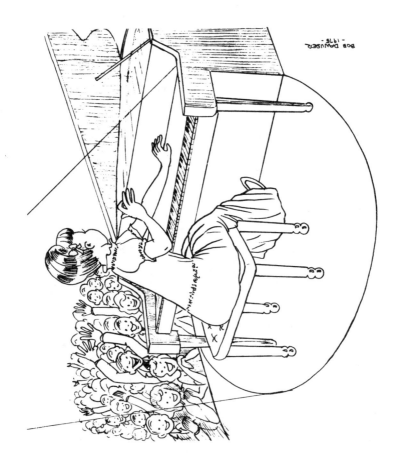

BOB DAWSER - 1975 -

"Oh, she doesn't intend to be mean," Nancy answered. "She really cares, and wants us to do it right. I really do want to learn to play the piano, and Mother says Mrs. Thompson is the best teacher in Proverbsville."

"She's so old, her head shakes," Judy said scornfully. "And lots of times I like my way better than her way."

"But she's the teacher, so we ought to do it her way."

Judy shook her head. "Not me. I get tired of hearing how badly I play."

Nancy sighed. "I have to admit—I'm so tired of Chopin's Polonaise in A Major I hope I never hear it again—after the contest, I mean," she added hastily.

"Oh, Nancy, who do you think will win? Maybe you or me? Wouldn't that be fun? All the kids in school will be there. And the winner gets her picture in the *Daily Journal*, and you get interviewed on television, and everything!"

"Your piece sounded very pretty, Judy. Maybe you'll win."

Judy beamed. "Oh, I hope so. That would prove to nasty old Mrs. Thompson I'm not so dumb after all."

Nancy put her hand on Judy's arm. "Maybe you shouldn't talk that way, Judy. Remember our memory verse from last Sunday: 'Surely he scorneth the scorners: but he giveth grace unto the lowly'—Proverbs 3:34? Remember that Miss Bixler told us God wants us to be meek instead of being 'know-it-alls'?"

Judy wrinkled her nose. "I don't like to be meek and lowly." She tossed her curly head. "I'm sure I know as much piano as Mrs. Thompson does, and frankly, I think Mother is wasting her money sending me to her."

But Nancy looked very thoughtful. " 'Meek' doesn't sound very exciting. . .but I sure don't want God to scorn me, either. So I'll just keep trying to be meek anyway."

Nancy's mother had made her a lovely long dress for the talent contest. That night her mother combed her hair and put it on top of her head. Nancy felt quite grown-up, even if all her muscles turned to Jello when she stepped out on the stage. Nancy couldn't see a thing—black specks seemed to float before her eyes. But her fingers had practiced so well, so faithfully, that they automatically, almost magically went to the right notes. A beautiful cascade of sound poured out of the grand piano.

Nancy stood, then curtsied. The kids clapped and cheered, and begged her to play her piece again. At the end of the program, the judges' decision was unanimous: Nancy Burdette had won the talent contest! Flash bulbs popped. People pulled at her, trying to shake her hand.

Dear Mrs. Thompson, her face flushed and happy, squeezed Nancy tight. "I'm so happy for you, dear. You earned this great honor. You were a teachable little girl."

"Thank you, thank you, Mrs. Thompson, for all you taught me."

"Now," Mrs. Thompson said briskly, "there's one place I wasn't quite satisfied with. You remember that trill at the top of the fourth page?"

Nancy giggled happily, and said, "Yes, Mrs. Thompson?"

13. What Happened to Eddie's New Jacket?

Those Generous Kids in Proverbsville

Eddie was riding his bike home from school when he noticed the car stopped right on the highway. That was a dangerous place to stop—must have engine trouble, or maybe they'd only run out of gas. He pedaled over to the car. It was a lady, with a carful of noisy kids. Eddie poked his helpful head through the window.

"Say, lady, you need gas? There's a gas station back a block. Want me to get some gas for you?"

The woman turned and stared at Eddie. He suddenly realized she'd been crying, "No," she mumbled, "no, thank you."

"Oh, is it car trouble?"

"No, it's only out of gas."

"Then I'll ride my bike and get you some."

The woman shook her head tiredly. "I don't have any money for gas."

"Oh. . . ." Eddie's thoughts raced. "Say, I'll go home and ask Mom for a couple of dollars."

"But I can't pay you back."

"Look, lady, it's dangerous for you to be here. Somebody might not see your car in time, and run into it. Let me help you shove it to the side of the road. Then you and the kids come with me to my house; see how cold they

are? I'll run get some gas, and then you can get home, at least."

Eddie pushed his bike along side the pitiful little family as they walked toward the house. Their name was Robinson. Mr. Robinson was in the hospital, had been for months, had been there so long the insurance and unemployment compensation had all run out. Gerald, here—he was fourteen—had quit school so he could help earn money, but in this weather nobody needed much yard work done, and that was about all he could do. They were on their way to the welfare office to see if maybe they could get help there, when the car conked out.

Eddie eyed Gerald. "You really fourteen?"

"Yep."

Hmm, Eddie thought. Must be the poor food: Gerald wasn't as tall as he, and Eddie was only eleven! They must have been hungry for a very long time. "Don't worry," he said aloud, "my mom will know what to do—and she won't mind a bit my bringing you all home."

And she didn't! She acted as if it were perfectly normal to have four extra, frightened, hungry, poorly-dressed guests for supper without any notice at all!

After supper, Mother asked the Robinsons to rest in the living room, since she had a few chores to do before she took them home. Eddie knew what she was planning. She'd go to the pantry and fill up a couple of sacks with nourishing food. Then she'd see what clothes she could find to give the family so they'd be warm for a while, anyway.

Sure enough, Eddie found her in the kitchen pantry. "Mom, did you notice, Gerald doesn't have a jacket of any kind on?"

"I noticed that, Eddie. What did you have in mind?"

"Well, uh, would it hurt your feelings if I gave my new jacket to him? I know you paid a lot of money for it. But I hate to see that guy so cold."

"But, Eddie, what would you wear?"

"My old jacket."

"But it's too little—that's why we bought the new one. Why not give him your old jacket?"

Eddie hung his head. "Oh, I dunno. It seemed like if I were going to give him something, it would be sort of like giving it to Jesus, and so I wanted it to be my best. You remember that verse you are always quoting, Mother?"

His mother smiled. "I remember: 'He that hath pity upon the poor lendeth unto the Lord; and that which he hath given will he pay him again'—Proverbs 19:17. But, Son, we can't afford to buy you another new jacket. You'll have to get by this winter with the old one."

"Suits me fine," Eddie said cheerfully.

That night, when the Clevelands took the Robinson family home, Eddie gave Gerald his neat brown sports jacket. Eddie stood there in his beat-up jacket, his arms dangling from the too-short sleeves. But things seemed all mixed up, for Eddie looked like the happiest person in the whole room! And maybe he was.

14. Carol Makes a Bargain With the Principal

Those Confident Kids in Proverbsville

When Miss Sullivan assigned the book report, all the boys in the class groaned, but Carol sighed happily. She loved to read, and it was most fun when you had a good excuse for reading, like when it was assigned homework. Carol checked the book out of the library that very day. That night she tucked the book under her arm, balanced her Coke and dill pickle and bologna sandwich in both hands, and headed for her favorite chair in the living room for a cozy evening of reading.

It was a book she'd never heard of, but that wasn't surprising. There must be thousands of books in the world she hadn't read yet—but she was having fun working on the pile! She hoped this book would be a good one, one that she could read again and again and enjoy just as much every time she read it. She opened to the first page and began to read.

But when she'd read a few paragraphs, she squeezed her eyes closed and snapped the book shut. Then she cautiously opened the book again, as if maybe she'd read something that wasn't there. She turned the pages over swiftly, then slammed the book shut again. Her face was pale with shame when she brought it to her father. "Daddy, this is the book Miss Sullivan assigned for our book report."

Her father looked at her stricken face. "Is something wrong with it?"

"Oh, Daddy, it has the awfullest words in it. The people use bad words, and do wicked things. It makes me feel dirty all over."

"Then don't read it," her father said quietly. "Choose another book."

"I can't," Carol said miserably. "Everybody in the class is supposed to read this book."

"I am sure Miss Sullivan will be happy to assign another book for you, Carol. I'll write an excuse for you. If you'd like, I'll talk to her for you."

"No, sir, I can do it. And thank you, Daddy."

But Miss Sullivan wasn't happy to assign another book. She arched her eyebrows and tilted her chin. In a voice the whole class could hear she said, "What do you mean, you can't read this book?"

Carol heard the kids snicker. "It's full of bad words," she stammered, "and the people do such wicked things."

Miss Sullivan smiled graciously. "Carol, that is life. This book describes how real teenagers feel. That's the way life really is. This is honest writing."

Carol's eyes filled with tears. "Then I don't want to read honest writing. Please, can I read something else?"

"No," Miss Sullivan said firmly. "You can't discuss this book with the class if you haven't read it."

"But my father said—"

"I'm sure your father will understand when you explain it to him."

But Father didn't understand, not at all! "No, Carol, you will not read that book. I'll take you out of school before I'll let them make you read that garbage. But before that, let's see if we can't find some way to do right and still please Miss Sullivan."

"Maybe I could offer to read two books instead of one."

"Good idea! Don't be afraid, Carol. The Lord will help you. 'The Lord shall be thy confidence,' Proverbs 3:26 says. And Proverbs 28:1 says, 'The wicked flee when no man pursueth: but the righteous are bold as a lion.' When you are doing right, you don't have to be afraid of anyone. Be courteous and obedient, and find some way to please them without doing wrong. . . .Would you like for me to go to school with you tomorrow?"

"No, sir, I can handle it," Carol said bravely.

But the next morning Miss Sullivan was as hard as a concrete block. "Read this book, or go see the principal."

Carol was trembling when she knocked on Mr. Walker's door, but he answered pleasantly. Evidently Miss Sullivan had already talked to him, for he said, "Carol, you've always been a cooperative little girl. We've never had trouble with you before. Why don't you just give up and read the book Miss Sullivan wants you to read?"

Carol wrinkled her nose. "Have you read it, Mr. Walker? It's *awful.*"

"Be honest with me, Carol. Aren't you doing this because your father is making you do it?"

Carol shook her head firmly. "No, sir, I'm the one who went to him and asked him to help me. . . .Look, Mr. Walker, you've got a whole room full of books here. Aren't any of them good? Wouldn't any of them help me be a good girl instead of putting bad things in my mind? Look, pick out three of them, any three you know are good, and I'll read all three of them. Three good books for one dirty one—is it a deal?"

Mr. Walker chuckled aloud. "O.K., it's a deal. Here, take *Lorna Doone,* and *Kidnapped,* and *Little Women*—you've read it?—then take *The Scarlet Pimpernel.*"

Carol took the books happily. "And when I've finished these, if you have some more good ones, could you punish me some more by making me read them, too?" she teased.

Mr. Walker's face sobered. "Young lady, I'll personally see that no child in this school is required to read a book he believes will hurt him. I wish we had a school full of students as creative and confident as you!"

15. The Bully Sets a Trap for Matthew

Those Kind Kids in Proverbsville

Matthew stood in front of his father and cleared his throat nervously to catch his attention. His dad was reading the Proverbsville *Daily Journal*, and didn't seem to notice. Finally Matthew blurted out, "Say, Dad, can I talk to you?"

His father immediately put down the newspaper and pulled up a chair with his foot for Matthew. "Sure, Son, what do you need?"

"I have a question about the Bible. You remember that place where Jesus said when somebody hits you on one cheek, you're supposed to turn the other cheek? Does a fellow always have to do that?"

His father's eyes softened. "Somebody been hitting you, Son?"

In spite of all Matthew could do, a big tear rolled down his cheek. "A guy at school. . .His name's Butch. He keeps picking fights. Even when I go home a different way after school, he catches me and tries to fight."

Father grunted. "This Butch, is he a pretty big guy? Hard to lick?"

Matthew nodded. "He'd skin me alive if he caught me."

A grin creased Father's tanned face. "Another piece of Bible advice says don't try to fight a fellow you can't whip (Luke 14:31,32). Of course, that doesn't mean you have to stand around and let him beat up on you. That's not what Matthew 5:39 means. If you've wronged somebody, then you ought to let them decide how to fix it. Have you wronged Butch? Made fun of him? Teased him?"

"No, sir; he's that way with everybody. Nobody likes him."

"Perhaps I should talk to his father."

"He doesn't have a father, Dad. His mother works in a bar at night, so she's not there when he's home. Besides, he doesn't pay much attention to her anyway."

"Have you tried being kind to him? Maybe he's a bully to cover up how he really feels."

"Yes, sir," Matthew sighed, "I've tried being kind. The other day he was lying in the street, his bike on top of him. I thought he was hurt and ran over to help him up. He jumped up, and laughed, and started chasing me again—it was just a trick."

"Butch needs the Lord," Father said gravely. "Matthew, you're going to have to help him find Him. Proverbs 10:12 says, 'Hatred stirs up strifes: but love covers all sins.' Why don't you ignore Butch's behavior, and set out to be his friend? Then he won't have to prove how great he is. See if you can win his respect by showing him true Christian love. If you have to, go ahead and fight him—but try the other way first."

The next day Butch disappeared right after school. Matthew sighed with relief, but just for safety, decided to walk a different way home from school. It was a long way home, out past the old Olson house—the haunted house, the kids called it, because it was so old and rotten and falling down. It was worth walking a long way just to keep from running into mean old Butch!

But just as Matthew got near the old Olson house, he heard a voice screaming, "Help me! Oh, somebody, please help me!"

Matthew gulped and ran toward the house. Somebody was in terrible trouble! "Help me!" the voice cried again, "I'm trapped!"

Then Matthew's feet skidded to a stop all by themselves. That sounded like Butch's voice. Matthew crept forward. Sure enough, it was Butch, lying under a pile of boards inside the Olson house. The sign said, "Keep Out"—so why was Butch there? Maybe he's stacked that pile of lumber on himself, just to trap Matthew. But how had he known Matthew was coming this way? Had he followed him, then run ahead? "It's a trick," Matthew thought grimly.

Then Butch spied Matthew. "Please help me! I'm caught."

"It's another trap," Matthew argued with himself. "I'd be a fool to let him trick me twice with the same trick. . . .But what if he really is hurt, and can't get help? Nobody else is around. Should I? Oh, I don't know what to do!"

"Matthew, please—it hurts!" Butch's head sagged, and his eyes fell shut.

Then Matthew remembered what his father had said: "Show Butch true Christian love." "I'll do it," Matthew decided, "even if it kills me—but Lord, will You help me?"

Matthew ran down the sidewalk, leaped up the steps, and started pulling off the rotten boards. One huge beam really was jammed. Matthew couldn't budge it. He found another board, and pried it up just enough so Butch could squeeze out from under it.

Butch stood up, his legs trembling with fatigue. He wiped the sweat and dirt off his hands, and held out a hand to Matthew. "Thanks, Buddy. You were a real sport to do that for me after the nasty way I've treated you."

"Aw, that's O.K.," Matthew answered. And it really was, for one night, not many weeks later, Matthew's father led Butch to the Lord Jesus.

16. Is It Any Use Trying to Help Kevin?

Those Patient Kids in Proverbsville

Karen touched the doorbell, then stepped back nervously. Could she handle this job she'd volunteered for? The door opened. "Mrs. Parker?" Karen asked. "I'm Karen Hughes. From Miss Thompson's sixth-grade class. She said you need some help with your little boy."

Mrs. Parker's troubled face lighted up—she was much prettier, much younger-looking when she smiled. "Come in, Karen. Miss Thompson told me you were coming. I'm very grateful that you and the other girls in the class have volunteered to help us with Kevin. Before you meet him, let me tell you about him. He was born with cerebral palsy. He can't take care of himself, can't walk, can't even sit up alone, though he's five years old.

"Oh," Karen mourned. "I'm sorry. How can I help?"

"The doctor has given us certain exercises for Kevin. If we'll move his arms and legs every day in certain patterns, perhaps some day he'll learn to make his muscles do what his mind tells them to do."

"Does he like the exercises?"

"Kevin can't talk, Karen. We don't know whether it's because his brain is damaged, or whether he just can't get across the barrier of his damaged nerves and muscles."

Karen sucked in her breath. "Oh, I'll help all I can!"

"Thank you, Karen. But Kevin is sometimes difficult to

71

work with. He drools, and his head flops around. Some of the girls have gotten discouraged—he seems so hopeless."

"I didn't expect it to be easy," Karen answered quietly.

"You're a sweet girl. Now come and meet Kevin."

Kevin didn't seem to notice Karen. He lay on his back on the bed, his head rolling from side to side, his arms and legs thrashing.

"We put him on the floor like this," Mrs. Parker explained. "Now take this arm, and this leg, move them forward, then back, in rhythm—just like he were swimming. Then take the other arm and leg and move them forward and back."

"Oh, I can do that."

"He needs to do it for 20 minutes at a time. You can talk to him while you do it, but keep the rhythm steady."

"Watch me and see if I do it right. . . . One, two, three, four. Forward, back, forward, back."

"That's fine, Karen. I'll be in the kitchen if you need me."

Karen talked to Kevin as she worked, "Forward, back, forward, back, one, two, three, four." Then she started making up little songs to help pass the time. "Dear little Kevin, move your leg, and your arm, now the other leg and arm. . . . Karen loves Kevin. Does Kevin love Karen? . . . Someday you'll grow to be big and strong. . . ."

Week after week Karen came to the Parker home. Week after week she pushed and pulled, sang and cajoled. "But it doesn't seem to do any good," she wailed.

"Don't get discouraged," Mrs. Parker said. "If Kevin ever makes one deliberate movement, trying to help you, if he ever says one word, then we'll know there's hope."

But weeks went by, and Kevin hardly seemed to notice

her. His thin little legs jerked out of her grip, and he'd never once seemed to try.

One day Karen threw herself into her mother's arms. "Oh, Mommy, it's no use. Kevin's never going to get better. He's always going to be just a blob—and it hurts so bad I can hardly stand it."

Mother didn't fuss at her brokenhearted little girl. "It seems that way, Karen. But you are doing all you can do, and that's all God expects."

"I don't see why God let him even be born."

"Does his mother say that?"

"Oh, no, she loves him, and never gives up hope."

"And that's what you must do. Remember Proverbs 13:12 says, 'Hope deferred maketh the heart sick; but when the desire cometh, it is a tree of life.' When God finally answers your prayers and rewards your hard work, aren't you going to be glad you were patient?"

Karen wiped the tears out of her eyes. "O.K., Mom, I'll keep working."

And she did, week after week. "One, two, three, four, forward, back, forward, back. . .Karen loves Kevin. Does Kevin love Karen?"

One day as she lifted him from the floor and put him back in bed, she looked into his vacant eyes and squeezed him tight. "Oh, Kevin," she whispered, "Karen really loves Kevin. Does Kevin love Karen?"

A glimmer of light came into Kevin's dark eyes. His lips twitched. Then the words stumbled out, one at a time but clear enough that Karen could understand them even above the hard beating of her heart: "Kevin loves Karen!"

17. What Could Be More Dangerous Than a Car Smash-up?

Those Pure Kids in Proverbsville

Mrs. Harding hung up the phone and sighed. "That was your father. He's bringing the Hansens home for a snack—and I haven't a thing in the house!"

"Mom, make one of those scrumptious coffee cakes, all buttery and cinnamony like only you can make," her son Pete said.

She tousled his hair. "Flatterer! I can't. There's not a drop of milk in the house, and the supermarket is closed."

"What about that new little grocery store that stays open all night? I could hop on my bike and be back in ten minutes."

"Well, I don't like for you to be on your bike at night."

"Shucks, Mom, I'm twelve years old. It's only 8:00 o'clock. I've got lights on my bike, and reflector tapes. I won't get hurt."

"All right. Here's the money. Buy me one gallon, please."

Mrs. Harding didn't think to warn Pete of something much more dangerous than a careening car on a darkened street, something that could hurt Pete much more permanently than any bicycle accident.

The store looked new and shiny. Pete found the cooler where the milk was, picked up a gallon, paid the man for

it, and started out the door. Right by the front door his eye caught a rack of magazines. On the front of one was a stunning picture of a motorcycle—a Harley-Davidson, with 1200 c.c.'s—screaming along the curve of a highway through a mountain pass. Pete grabbed up the magazine—someday he'd do that, he thought, own a Harley-Davidson just like that. Without thinking, Pete put down the milk, and opened to the story inside. When he flipped the magazine open, though, he discovered it had more pictures of girls in it than it did of motorcycles. And none of them were dressed like a girl ought to dress.

Pete had never seen pictures like that. He didn't dream anybody would want to look at that kind of pictures. Pete's father was a good man. He never told shady stories, never used bad language, never talked disrespectfully about girls. He had taught Pete to be careful, too, to control what went into his mind. "As a man thinketh in his heart, so is he" (Prov. 23:7)," Pete's daddy would often quote.

So Pete hadn't picked the magazine up on purpose to look at the dirty pictures. But he held that magazine in his hands two minutes longer than he should have. Some of those pictures burned themselves into his mind. Then, ashamed of himself, he flung the magazine back in the rack, grabbed his milk, leaped on his bike and pedaled home.

But the poisoned weed began to grow in his mind. Sometimes, studying in the evening, he'd remember what he'd seen. Or at school, during a class, a picture flashed into his mind. Then one terrible Sunday morning, while Pete's teacher was teaching the Sunday school lesson, Pete began to think about one of those pictures. He forgot all about being in class as he sat there, imagining. Suddenly he woke up, like from a dream, hearing his Sunday school teacher asking, "Pete, do you know it?"

"Know what, sir?" Pete mumbled.

The boys tittered. Usually Pete knew all the answers.

"Our memory verse," the teacher answered patiently.

"Uh, no, sir."

"Todd, can you quote it?"

"Yes, sir: 'The thoughts of the wicked are an abomination to the Lord: but the words of the pure are pleasant words' (Proverbs 15:26)."

Pete listened to the words, and sickened with shame. How wicked it had been to sit in church and think the thoughts he'd been thinking! Why, he'd practically made a garbage can out of his mind, when his body was the temple of the Holy Spirit! Right then Pete forgot all about the class again. "O Lord," he prayed, "please forgive me. Help me get those wicked pictures out of my mind, and never, never do that again. Amen."

". . .Well, Pete, we're waiting!" the teacher was saying.

"Gulp! My turn again?" Pete roused himself and marshalled his thoughts. "O.K., it goes: 'The thoughts of the wicked are abomination to the Lord: but the words of the pure are pleasant words'—and you'll find it some place in that great book of Proverbs!" he ended gamely.

The class hooted, but Pete's teacher seemed to understand. "And can I find it written in your heart, Pete?" he asked quietly.

Pete looked into his eyes honestly. "Yes, sir. It is!"

18. Can Pam Trust God to Make Even Disgrace All Right?

Those Trusting Kids in Proverbsville

"Oh, Mrs. Edwards, now *my* five dollars is gone!" Susan gasped, when she opened her purse to pay for her lunch ticket. Everybody in the class groaned. It was the third time that week money had been stolen. You couldn't guess who the thief was, and since money looks the same, it wouldn't do any good to search the kids.

Mrs. Edwards bit her lip. Her eighth-grade class had always been a special place; kids hoped to be assigned to her because she loved to help you learn. But this ugly thing had wormed its way into the room, and now nobody could trust anybody.

Pam, Susan and Audrey were best friends, and they all looked dismayed. It gave you a panicky feeling to know that somebody you knew, somebody you smiled at, was smiling back and stealing from you when you weren't looking!

"Say, Mrs. Edwards," Susan said, "I could recognize my five-dollar bill. It was torn all the way down to Mr. Lincoln's nose, and Daddy Scotch taped it when he gave it to me this morning."

"Search us, Mrs. Edwards," the kids said. "We're tired of all this."

"No, I wouldn't like to do that," she said.

79

"But the thief ought to be caught," they insisted. And Mr. Walker, the principal, agreed. He came into the room to supervise the search.

When it came time for Audrey's purse to be searched, she flipped open the lid with a laugh, "Boy, I wish you *could* find $5.00 in my purse!" Pam laughed too, when her purse was searched. But her laugh changed to a gasp as she watched Mrs. Edwards pull out a five-dollar bill, and unroll it slowly. Sure enough, it was taped in the middle, down to Mr. Lincoln's eye. Pam was Susan's best friend—and here was Susan's $5.00 in Pam's purse! "Oh, Pam, how could you?" Audrey wailed.

Pam could hardly talk for sobbing. "It's a joke. Somebody put it there—look, I didn't take it. I wouldn't steal. Mrs. Edwards, you know I wouldn't take that money."

Everybody was shocked. Pam had always seemed to be a good Christian girl. She went to Sunday school and church; she begged the other kids to come too. At school she studied hard, and made good grades. She was an enthusiastic cheerleader at the basketball games. You could always count on Pam. It was hard to believe—but it must be true: Pam was a thief!

There were two people in the room that day who knew the truth: Pam, and the girl who had stolen the money. And that girl wasn't talking!

Mr. Walker was kind but firm. Pam couldn't be a cheerleader. She couldn't attend any more social activities. She was on probation for the rest of the semester.

Pam thought her heart would break. Even her best friends, Audrey and Susan, shunned her. Daddy and Mother believed her, but they were her parents, so that didn't seem to count. Day after day she'd pray, "Lord, please, *please*, let people find out I'm not a thief."

"Mother," Pam said, "sometimes I feel like doing something real mean to those folks—it's not fair for them to do this to me!"

"No, Pam, you can't do that," her mother answered gently.

"I wish I could crawl into a deep dark hole and die!"

Mother put her arms around Pam. "Honey, Proverbs 3:5 and 6 has the answer for you: 'Trust in the Lord with all thine heart, and lean not unto thine own understanding: In all thy ways acknowledge him and he shall direct thy paths.' The Lord says for you not to trust your own judgment but to trust Him and He will make it right. Honey, it's up to you. You've been wronged. Are you going to keep on worrying and fretting, or are you going to let God make it turn out all right?"

"But it's so unfair!"

"Not if God is in control. What are you going to do?" Mother insisted.

Pam put her head in her hands. "I'm going to trust Him!"

Nothing seemed to change. Things still disappeared in the classroom: lunch money, Alfred's silver dollar from his coin collection, Ralph's expensive ballpoint pen. They were never found. The kids would look at Pam suspiciously, and she could only shrug helplessly. All she could do was trust God. And finally God did take charge.

One day Audrey and Susan came into class giggling and joking. Audrey carried a stack of books with her purse on top. Just as she reached her desk, she tripped over Ralph's big foot. "Ralph, you clumsy oaf!" she complained, as

books and papers rained down and things spilled from her purse.

Ralph reddened, and jumped up to help her pick things up. He picked up a ballpoint pen, and stared at it. "Audrey, this is my pen," he said quietly.

"Don't be silly, Ralph; there are hundred of pens like that."

"Not with my initials engraved on them."

Audrey grabbed the pen and her eyes widened. "I never saw that," she whispered miserably. And soon the whole sorry story tumbled out. She was the one who stole the money, and the pen, and the silver dollar. When she realized she was about to be caught with Susan's $5.00 bill, she had rolled it up tight and slipped it under the cover of Pam's purse while they stood in line to be searched.

Pam was crying again. "Oh, Audrey, why? I was your friend."

"I know," Audrey answered miserably. "Will you forgive me? Please don't be angry with me."

"How can I be angry," Pam said softly, "when I've just learned I really can trust God to do right about everything?"

19. How Can Teddy Be Happy When He Lost the Race?

Those Self-Controlled Kids in Proverbsville

Teddy sprawled on the floor, reading the Proverbsville *Daily Journal*. "Hey, Dad, what's a soap box derby?"

His father knelt by Teddy and read the news item. "It's a race where kids drive cars they build. They make them out of wooden crates like boxes soap was packed in."

"What makes them go? A motor?"

"No, gravity. You coast down a hill."

"I see—they're using Foley's Mountain. Dad, the winner of this derby gets a prize of $300.00." Teddy's eyes closed dreamily. "That would pay a whole semester for me at the Christian school, wouldn't it?"

"I do wish you could go to the Christian school, Teddy. But with this new business, I have to keep putting back every penny of profit. I couldn't even pay your second semester if you won enough to pay the first."

"Maybe another contest will come along by then," Teddy grinned.

"O.K., try it. I'll help all I can."

Teddy's father took him to the library to get some books on building a soap box car, and on aerodynamics, so he could make a good design that would cut down wind resistance. Teddy took the wheels from an old wagon and worked out a clever way to steer it and brake it. Every day as Teddy worked on the cart, he prayed the Lord would help him win so he could go to the Christian school.

Teddy took it for a test drive out on Foley's Mountain, and it skimmed down the road as if powered by an eight-cylinder motor! The wind sang in his ears, and Teddy thought sure he could win that race. But in the pre-trial heat, Teddy crossed the finish line at the very same time a boy named Keith did. The officials let them try again, and again they were neck-and-neck all the way down the hill to the goal. They knew they were well-matched, and that it would be a tight race between them.

"I'll smear you," Keith threatened.

"Not if I can help it," Teddy answered sturdily.

"I'm going to win that money no matter what it takes," Keith retorted.

The whole town of Proverbsville, it seemed, was out for the race on a hot July morning. The finalists lined up nervously, blowing on their hands and shuffling their feet, as if that would help their cars go faster.

The starting gun fired. The drivers snapped off their brakes. The cars began their slow roll down the hill. Teddy and Keith's cars immediately passed the others. They gathered momentum and soon were streaking down the long hill. Teddy leaned forward, straining with all his might to keep in the center of his lane, to make no sideways motion that would slow him down or disqualify him by getting out of his lane. Keith's jaunty red and white job stayed right alongside, as if joined by an invisible wire. Teddy's mouth was dry. Spots floated in front of his eyes as the white "finish" banner loomed into view.

Suddenly, Keith pointed and screamed, "LOOK OUT! Don't hit it!" Teddy jerked the wheel, afraid a child had

run out on the road. Then he could see: there was nothing there. He had been tricked! Keith had deliberately driven him out of his lane so he would be disqualified! Keith won the race, and no one seemed to realized he had cheated to win it!

The judge was apologetic but firm. "I'm sorry, Son. We have to stick by the rules. You are disqualified because you got out of your lane, no matter for what reason. Keith Jones is the winner!"

It was wrong, wrong, wrong! Hot tears burned Teddy's eyes. He felt like yelling, to tell everybody how unfair it was. "But I can't do that," he thought miserably, "I can't lose my temper just because somebody else does wrong." He clamped his lips tight, to keep the angry words from spilling out. Quietly he wheeled his racer through the spectators. A businessman put a hand on his shoulder. "Say, Son, what happened back there? Why did you swerve?"

"I thought a child had gotten into the road."

"You were tricked, weren't you?"

"Yes, sir."

"You had a right to be angry. I could see you get hold of yourself and decide not to be angry. Why?"

Teddy's face lighted up with a bleak grin. "Because my dad taught me Proverbs 16:32, *'He that is slow to anger is better than the mighty and he that ruleth his spirit than he that taketh a city.'*"

The man pulled out a business card. "I'm Stanford Wilson, editor of the Proverbsville *Daily Journal*. I need a boy with the kind of self-discipline you displayed today. Want a job?"

"Sure! Doing what?"

"Be a copy boy at the paper for me. Afternoons after school and Saturday. I'll pay you minimum wage. You could earn maybe $20.00 a week. Talk it over with your parents and see what they say."

"Wow! Oh, that's better than winning the race, because now I can go to the Christian school. Whoopee! Thank you, thank you, sir!"

"Thank *you*, young man. You've made my day. I didn't know we had any kids like you left in America!"

"Aw, Proverbsville's full of 'em," Teddy said modestly, "—but I'm glad it's me you want!"

20. Why Couldn't Tony Go to Sunday School?

Those Obedient Kids in Proverbsville

"Wow! Am I glad I came to Sunday school today!" Tony said to himself as he squeezed onto a bench already crowded with sixth graders. It was fun to come to this church. The Sunday school teacher, Mr. Brown, seemed to be glad to see all the kids. When Mr. Brown prayed, Tony kept one eye opened, and squinted around the room, because the teacher made it sound like he was talking with God, and God was right there in the room listening. When the teacher opened his Bible and told how much Jesus loved Tony, and died on the cross so Tony could be forgiven for his sins, and go to Heaven, Tony thought, "That's what I want!"

Tony's hand was the first to shoot up when the teacher asked who wanted to be saved. After class was over, Mr. Brown explained it all again, since it was the first time Tony had ridden the bus to Sunday school. Then Tony talked to God himself—yes, he did—Tony actually talked out loud to God, and God heard him and saved him, like He promised He would!

After Tony got saved, he grinned at Mr. Brown. "You can bet I'll be back next Sunday and every Sunday, if I can sneak out of the house so my old man doesn't catch me."

"Hey, didn't your father give you permission to come today?"

"Shucks, no. He wouldn't let me out of the house to go to church! Why, if he finds out I went to church this morning, he'll whale the tar out of me!"

"Now that would be a catastrophe!" Mr. Brown agreed. "But, Tony, now that you belong to the Lord, you're going to have to do what He tells you to do. Guess what the very first thing is that God wants you to do?"

"Quit stealing and quit swearing," Tony replied promptly.

"Well, yes, that, too. But the first thing is to obey your father and mother. Proverbs 6:20 and 21 says, 'My son, keep thy father's commandment, and forsake not the law of thy mother: Bind them continually upon thine heart, and tie them about thy neck.' So how about asking permission next Sunday before you come to church?"

Tony scratched his head. "But why wouldn't it be right for me to go to church? My goodness, how can I be a good Christian if I can't even go to church?"

Mr. Brown's voice was very gentle. "Tony, you be a good Christian by obeying your folks, and God will see to it that you get to go to church."

"Aw, all right, I'll try it."

Sometimes Tony got to go, and sometimes he didn't. Sometimes Mr. Goldoni was so drunk he didn't care what Tony did. Other times he would curse and swear at Tony, and forbid him to ride the bus to Sunday school.

Nearly every Saturday Tony's Sunday school teacher would drop by. Often Mr. Goldoni was rude to him, and Tony would be afraid Mr. Brown would get discouraged and quit coming, but he never did. When he came, he'd have a book or a tract, something Tony could read to help him learn what God wanted him to learn when he couldn't go to church.

One Sunday Tony was especially anxious to go to church. A famous baseball player was going to be there. All the Proverbsville kids had seen him playing in the big leagues on television. He was going to be at church to tell how he got saved. Tony got up early Sunday, dressed, cleaned his room, helped his mom with breakfast so there wouldn't be an excuse for him not to go to church. But when he asked his father, Mr. Goldoni swore at him. "No, you can't go, never again. I'm tired of all that Christian talk. Now shut up and leave me alone."

It was all Tony could do to keep from bursting into tears, but all he said was, "Yes, sir." When the bus stopped at the door, he waved it on. Long after it was out of sight, Tony stared out the living room window.

Tony heard a gruff voice behind him. "Hey, kid, you really want to go to church today?"

"Yes, sir."

"How come you didn't sneak out like you usta?"

"My Sunday school teacher told me that was wrong."

His father pushed himself up out of the chair. "Well, I guess maybe I can take you down. . . .Lemme get a shirt on."

Tony couldn't think of a single word to say until they got to the church. Then he threw his arms around his dad. "Thanks, Dad. Why don't you stay?" But his father just grunted, and drove away.

The baseball hero was as exciting as Tony hoped he'd be. Between Sunday school and church, he got his autograph. During the service, Tony soaked in all the

singing and praying and preaching. Just think! He got to
come to church after all, and his own dad brought him! But
the best part came at the end of the service, after the
invitation, when the preacher had the folks stand up who
had come forward to be saved.

"Mr. Joseph Goldoni, would you please stand?"

Tony's head jerked up. His dad? His dad in the service?
Saved? What happened?

"Mr. Goldoni, who brought you to church today?"

"I brought my kid, and got curious, and decided to
stay."

"And you today have trusted Christ to be your
Saviour?"

"Yeah. It was my kid Tony really. He usta always steal
and lie and talk back to me, and since he got saved, he
doesn't. I figure if God can help a boy like Tony, He can
help a bad sinner like me!"

"Yippee!" Tony yelled joyfully, right out in the service.
Everybody smiled, thinking maybe that was Tony's way of
saying, "Praise the Lord!"—and maybe the Lord thought
so, too.